MW00676088

The
Selling Machine

The
Selling Machine

Michael Cannon, Michael Pace,
and Landy Wingard

New Model Publishing

For more information please visit,

www.thesellingmachine.net

Book design by,

Arbor Books, Inc.
19 Spear Road, Suite 202
Ramsey, NJ 07446

www.arborbooks.com

Printed in Canada

The Selling Machine
Michael Cannon, Michael Pace, and Landy Wingard.

1. Title 2. Author 3. Business/Marketing & Sales

Library of Congress Control Number: 2006926565
ISBN: 0-9785855-0-X

TABLE OF CONTENTS

The Selling Machine

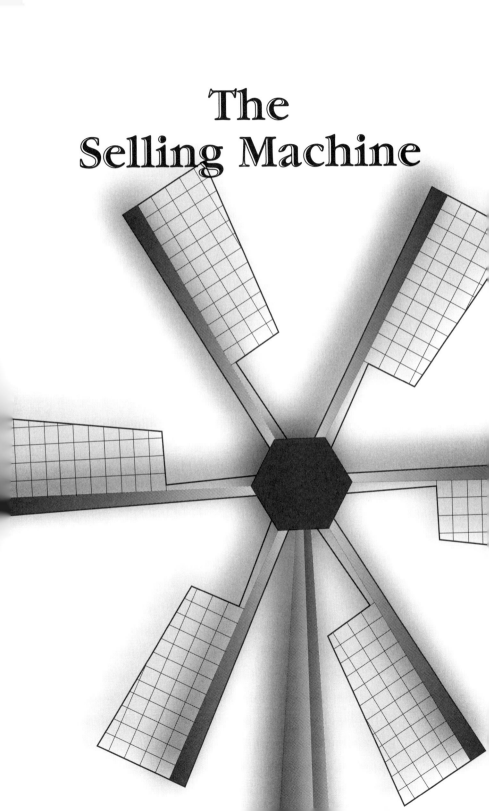

And looking back through my work, I see that it is invariably where I lacked a political purpose that I wrote lifeless books and was betrayed into purple passages, sentences without meaning, decorative adjectives and humbug generally.

George Orwell

INTRODUCTION

The Selling Machine was written as a response to the flawed assumptions and practices at work in today's sales world; flaws ultimately leading to poor customer service and marginalization of the sales profession. Our purpose in writing this book is to replace these flawed assumptions and practices for the benefit of those who choose to pursue selling as a career. Specifically, we want to move from a personality only approach to a complete sales process; from sales tricks and gimmickry to sales mastery and professionalism; from tension to teamwork; from feast or famine sales results to a repeatable business model; and ultimately, from poor or average to excellent customer service.

The Selling Machine is not just for the career salesperson. It applies to any person or company that has an idea, service or product to sell. If you are a salesperson, manager, business executive or entrepreneur, you will benefit from reading this book. If you are starting a new or second business, or if you are a displaced worker looking for innovative ways to market yourself, this book has value. It describes an adaptable and repeatable sales process that has been proven in the real world to increase sales and margins. It is practical in that it deals with the "blocking and tackling" of selling as opposed to mere theory.

There are no short-cuts to success. Success that endures is not a matter of chance, but the result of hard work. The point of a machine is to make that work productive, efficient and repeatable. The Selling Machine is a system designed to help you and your team stay on track with your sales work, and help you become even more successful by providing proven tactics and insights into the competitive world of sales.

Working smart and working hard are the two surest ways of being successful in the sales field. We are all born with certain traits and some of us may even be blessed with what can be called a sales personality. You may be the kind of person who people regard as a natural salesperson. There are many profile techniques used to identify a certain kind of personality type that is supposed to produce success in the sales field. Once in the sales trenches, however, one quickly realizes that success in sales depends upon more than these natural gifts. You need a system.

The sales profession is widely regarded as more of an art than a science like medicine or engineering. To some extent this is true. It is a mistake, however, to think of it as only an art. In many ways selling resembles military or political science: a blending between art and science involving strategy and persuasion. It is a mistake to assume that some degree of science cannot be applied to selling. The Selling Machine is a start-to-finish sales system that provides a scientific framework to underpin the ancient art of selling.

In the mid 17th century, English military leader Oliver Cromwell dominated the British Isles with his "New Model Army." Cromwell's New Model represented an improved way of waging war that combined a systematic approach and coherent philosophy. In contrast to other armies of the time which tended to rely on charismatic leadership and individual heroism, and whose officer ranks were filled by the social elite, Cromwell created an organized and disciplined fighting machine based on merit.

All aspects of warfare were addressed in the New Model. Whether it involved fighting tactics or the supply chain, Cromwell had a reliable and repeatable system which was the main reason for his consistent success. Similarly, the emphasis on training and discipline made Cromwell's a thoroughly professional army. As a consequence, he was never once defeated in battle! The Selling Machine seeks to be for selling what the New Model was for fighting.

Another highly effective machine is the windmill. Long ago, humans figured out they could harness the power of wind to perform work. The sails of a windmill turn an axel which can then be used to grind grain into flour, pump water, or create electricity. It is amazing that such a simple machine can perform such important work. Because the windmill is such an effective machine, it is still in use today. You will notice throughout the book that the windmill is used as a unifying graphical illustration that helps organize and communicate the major principles of The Selling Machine.

We use this metaphor in order to illustrate the point that selling can be approached scientifically, and that when this approach is properly understood it can be applied in a systematic, and repeatable way, like a machine. We in no way mean to imply that by adopting this methodology you will become some kind of

THE SELLING MACHINE

clone, or that your interpersonal skills have less value. To the contrary, The Selling Machine is a tool that will leverage your strengths and free you from rote, mechanical, and unproductive sales behavior.

Every machine must be designed from beginning to end to produce the desired output based on the inputs and energy applied. The object of The Selling Machine is a consistent flow of sales. You will notice that the use of the suffix --ing is prevalent throughout the book. The dictionary defines --ing as denoting "an action, process, or art." We chose to use the active verb form in describing each step in the process in order to emphasize the active nature of selling. The six phases of The Selling Machine are actions that you as a salesperson take. YOU are The Selling Machine! Let's get started.

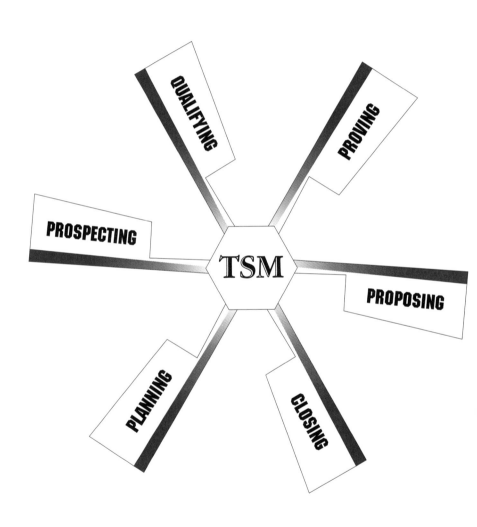

Discipline is the soul of an army. It makes small numbers formidable; procures success to the weak, and esteem to all.

George Washington

PLANNING

The first step in any consistently successful endeavor is planning. Planning is the single most important activity to becoming a selling machine yet it is without a doubt the least performed. Would you consider running a marathon without a strategy? Would you climb a mountain or start a company without drawing up a detailed plan? The answer to all theses questions is of course, 'No'. Selling is no different than running a marathon, climbing a mountain, or starting a company, in that planning is the foundation for success.

Though your plan will change as it evolves, it will be the key activity that we turn to time and time again as we make our way through the sales process. We must remember to routinely return to the planning table as a discipline, in order to achieve repeatable selling success. The specific planning steps detailed below will help you clarify goals, manage time and channel effort. The result of this activity will be a plan: A known destination, a meaningful value message, an initial list of potential prospects (suspects) and an awareness of the competitive landscape.

Destination Known

A person's life history is immortalized in his or her obituary. As morose as it may sound at first, an obituary truly is the final tally of each and every life. It tells not only what we did with our lives but implies by omission what we have not done. An interesting exercise you may consider is to write your own now before someone else writes it for you later. It's a great way to focus on the changes you want to make in your life before it is etched in stone.

It's an exercise often used in spiritual contexts to promote introspection, but is rarely applied in the business world as a planning tool. Honestly appraise who you are and what you have done with your life to this point. Once you've written your obituary, it will become apparent to you the things that you have not accomplished, but want to do in your life, both personally and professionally. This exercise will have the effect of crystallizing those goals that are most important to you and add urgency to them.

Writing an obituary and sales planning are similar, in that they both begin with the destination. The end goal in sales planning is a customer who will not only buy from you once, but will buy on a continuous basis and help you find and develop more of the same. In short, the beginning and end of selling is the same thing—a successful customer. The Selling Machine is not satisfied with a one-time sale to a customer who may or may not be successful. The Selling Machine insists on a successful outcome because the destination is known.

Write Down Your Goals

The primary deliverable for Destination Known is a written list of goals. It is widely known that those who write down and review their goals daily achieve more than those who do not. When you define your goals, first consider what it is that motivates you. In sales, motivation is invariably related to sales volume and status. The two go hand in glove. In most companies, the ranking of salespeople is not based on how nice or punctual they are, or what a good team player they might be, or any other soft factor. Instead, sales ranking is always driven by sales production.

Where do you want to be in this ranking? If your goal is to be the "top gun" at your company, then write it down. If you want to be the top performer year after year, write that down also. Or, if you're just starting out in sales, what is your goal for climbing up the ladder? Do you want to be in the top half, top third, etc? All goals should be challenging, measurable, and realistic. The Selling Machine will give you the confidence to achieve your goals because it offers a system that is mapped to those same goals.

When stating your goals, it is not enough to say you want to be the best or first, or even in the top 20%. Take it a step further and put a number to the goal. So, if the top salesperson last year produced $1.2 million in sales, you can probably assume that you will have to at least produce that much to contend for the "top gun." Once you have written down your goal, then you must map this goal to your daily activities so that the goal can be attained.

The next exercise is mapping the goal to your daily activities. So, if your goal is $1.2 Million in sales, and the average sales price for your product is $100,000, then you now know that you will have to make 12 sales in the year to achieve your goal. Going further, 12 sales per year on average is equivalent to 3 sales per quarter or 1 sale per month. Breaking down the very large number into a more manageable one will give you regular milestones, and allow you to track your activities and manage your time to increase the odds of making your goal. As you progress further into The Selling Machine, you will routinely revisit goals and make adjustments to some or all of your activities, so that not only will the goal be achieved, but achieved over and over again. Your goal will set the basis for which activities you should perform on a daily basis. It's all about planning!

Meaningful Value Message

A meaningful value message is one that resonates with your prospects. Customers are thirsty for salespeople to communicate with them on concrete economic terms. All too often, however, vague phrases such as "Increased Efficiency," "Improved Operations," "Improved Visibility," "Saves Time" and the like are misused as value messages. These terms are too nebulous to be compelling in today's market. Instead, hit home with some very direct and meaningful value statements. A good message is one that is provable. In a business setting, customers are looking for value that they can count. This type of value will make itself known on one or more of the financial statements that the customer maintains. Consider this Picture Wheel of value messages as a starting point for planning and developing your own.

INCREASES

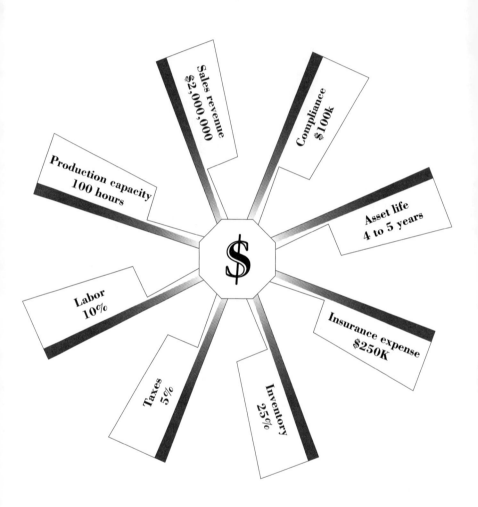

DECREASES

Note how all these examples are tangible and measurable. This is a key when working out your value messages. When selling to a business, the value proposition must be translated into dollars if it is to be compelling. This is different than the consumer sale which can revolve around such intangibles as status, comfort and convenience. It will take some work to translate what you sell into something as tangible as those listed, but it is an absolute necessity to becoming The Selling Machine.

The litmus test for your value message is whether or not it can be quantified. If your value message can be associated with quantifiable numbers then it will have meaning and power.

Begin and End With Your Customers

The Selling Machine is not about a churn and burn mentality. Your customers are your most valuable resource and must be treated as such. There is an old sales adage that goes, "if you take care of the customers you have, you will never have to worry about finding new ones." Therefore, first understand the customers you have. When analyzing your current customer base, document key characteristics such as company size, location, industry, who their customers are, how they operate, key decision makers, regulatory issues, etc.

Know how your product is being used, by whom, and what value it brings to their business. Be brutally honest in understanding your customers, so that you can determine whether or not they are successful. Are they successful? If so, why? In too many sales situations, a superficial dialogue goes something like this:

Salesperson: "How is everything going with the product I sold you, Earl?"

Customer: "Things are fine."

Salesperson: "So then you're happy with us?"

Customer: "Yes."

Usually that's the end of it. This kind of dialog between salespeople and customers does not get to the real issues. We need to go deeper and ask, "Why are you happy, and how exactly are you using the product?" "What tangible real benefits are you receiving?" Starting from where the last conversation ended, a better dialog would continue something like this.

Salesperson: "Why would you say you're happy?"

Customer: "The product seems to be working pretty well, no major problems."

Salesperson: "I see. So how exactly are you using the product and what features are most helpful?"

Customer: "Well, we use the inventory management feature daily and it seems to make things easier on the staff."

Salesperson: "That's good. How would you say it makes things easier?"

Customer: "They used to have to manually print stock reports and write down inventory, now it takes a lot less time, so the work gets done faster."

Salesperson: "Ah. That's really good. So from a management perspective would you say the investment you made with us was worth it?"

Customer: "Yes."

Salesperson: "Super. That's exactly what we wanted to hear. Tell me, have you been able to quantify exactly the time and money that the product has saved you?"

Customer: "Not exactly."

Salesperson: "Would you be open to me working with you to better understand the specifics?"

Customer: "Absolutely. My management has been asking me to do a report on the ROI that the product has produced compared to what we promised at the beginning when we bought it."

Salesperson: "Great. Let's set a follow up time for us to dig a little deeper."

Further, be open to problems and signs that the customer may not be successful. The traditional salesperson will shy away from the unhappy customer and consider him a distraction from closing the next sale. But knowing why a customer is successful or unsuccessful is a key to understanding our value proposition in the marketplace and the key to a solid selling plan. Remember, begin and end with your customers!

Initial List of Potential Prospects

Now that you know which customers are successful and why, the next task is to identify more of the same; in other words, define your playground. You need to identify what markets your customers are in, where they are located geographically, and their size— quantifiable in terms of number of employees, departmental budgets, annual revenue, market capitalization, population, square feet, number of locations, and subsidiaries. The key is to identify the distinguishing characteristics of your best customers and then find more.

Many sources can be used for this purpose. For instance, if you find that many of your most successful customers are regional hospitals with multiple locations in the Midwestern United States with employee size greater than 500, and number of beds at least 500, then you need to engage sources that can identify more hospitals with similar characteristics. The best and first place to start is always, without a doubt, your customers. If you have done a professional sales job and have built a consultative relationship with your customer, then you have earned the respect of your customer and the right to partner with him in the development of your selling plan.

A Strange Call

Usually customers call their salesperson when they have a problem or need information. Salespeople expect to get these routine calls. There is another kind of call that only the best salespeople get—like the guy who got a call from a customer asking him his opinion on some issues that seemed to have nothing to do with what he sold. He went to his sales manager to ask him what he thought. The sales manager knew instantly that this was a good sign and simply said, "Congratulations."

When the salesperson asked him to explain why he was congratulating him, the sales manager said, "Your customer has added you to his network, now add him to yours." "How do I do that?" The sales manager answered, "Ask him what associations he belongs to and join them, ask him what publications he sub-scribes to and read them." "Is there anything else?" the salesman asked. "Yes", said the sales manager. "Tell him you are doing account planning for the upcoming year and would like his help. Ask him who he knows that might be interested in obtaining the products and services you sell. Your customer will almost always be delighted to plug you into his network and offer refer-rals to his peers and recommend you to them."

You see, where most salespeople look at customer calls like this as a distraction or worse, a nuisance, The Selling Machine sees opportunity.

You may be asking yourself why this is the first and best place to start? Why are referrals more power-ful than any other lead source? The answer is simply that people buy things from people they like and trust.

Calls made into these referrals will always be warm because you will have the endorsement of one of their trusted peers. In short, this endorsement provides credibility. One of the core objectives of The Selling Machine, and the planning activities contained in it, is to put you in the position of never having to make another cold call.

Other Lead Sources

Another very useful source for building your list of potential prospects is the internet. There are subscription services such as Hoovers and One Source that, for a fee, will provide a software tool that allows users to quickly tailor searches and provide an initial potential prospect (suspect) list printout. There are other internet tools that will assist in the development of such a list free of charge. Though not as tailored or as quick, Google, Yahoo and other search engines fit this bill. There are also market associations and publications to consider. These can be very broad like the local Rotary or Kiwanis club or Chamber of Commerce directory, or industry-specific professional organizations and trade show attendee lists. Large lists of potential prospects can be gained from these sources.

A source often overlooked is your own personal network of family, friends and classmates. A good exercise is to write down a list of everyone you know and what they do for a living, where they live, and then call those that seem to make sense. You may be very pleasantly surprised to find that your Uncle Fred was once in the Army with the head of purchasing at a hospital that matches the profile you have defined.

In the end, the best salesperson may not always be the most persuasive (although that helps), but the one who best manages the various channels of in-flowing opportunity—lead sources.

By understanding your playground and using the sources mentioned, you should now have a list of potential prospects. These are only suspects at this point. The next step is to organize this list into an easy-to-use prioritized format. The Selling Machine believes that a Customer Resource Management (CRM) system is the most powerful tool to use in managing this information throughout the sales cycle and life cycle of that customer relationship. All of the information is right there and easily cross referenced to give you the ammunition and tools to deliver the highest level of customer service, and grow your sales pipeline. If a CRM is not available, a spreadsheet will also work with a bit more effort. Make sure you cross reference your list with your current customer list to remove duplicates. Below is an example of the type of information that is included in the initial list of potential prospects:

Company Name
Physical Address
Website
Main Phone Number
Revenue
Number of Employees
Lead Source

Now that we have an initial list of potential prospects, let's try to understand our competition.

Competitive Awareness

The process of understanding the competitive landscape is similar to developing a potential prospect list. Identify your top three competitors. Three is typically the maximum that the market will allow. Occasionally, you will come across a niche player not on your list, which will require you to revisit the Competitive Awareness process to develop a profile for that specific competitor.

There are many sources of information on your competitors. Again, the first and best sources are your customers. They will provide you the first-hand information that you need to develop your competitor profile. Customers can provide information not found on a website, document, product, or database. They will provide details that matter in building the relationship with the customer, such as whether the competitor is responsive or unresponsive, aggressive or professional, persistent or passive, consistent or inconsistent, as well as tell you about the tactics the competitor employs against your company.

Other places for gathering valuable information to round out your competitor profile are their website, internet search engines, subscription resources such as *Hoovers* and *Dun & Bradstreet*. Also, third party market analysts such as *Gartner Group, AMR, Consumer Reports* and others provide objective opinions on your product and company, as well as the competition. Set media alerts with *Google, Yahoo* and others so that you are up to date on current events involving your top competitors. If your competitor is a public company you should listen in on their quarterly earnings calls. There are also boutique firms that specialize in competitive intelligence. Another good place to find information is industry-specific publications that have done their own research and developed detailed studies of their own. All these help develop perspective regarding your strengths and weaknesses relative to those of your key competitors.

An example of the minimum details that you should include in your competitor profile:

Competitor's Name
Brief History of Company
Number of Employees
Sales Revenue
Profitability
Strategic Direction (Market Focus)
Strengths and Weaknesses of their Offering
Salesperson that is my Counterpart
Number of Customers
Best Customers
Products and Pricing Model

The resulting competitor profiles will be of recurring value as you position your solution in the proving and proposing stages discussed in subsequent chapters.

Many companies spend a great deal of time, effort, and funds not only on understanding their competitors, but seemingly in trying to mimic or even to turn themselves into clones. The Selling Machine approach, entitled, Competitive Awareness, chooses a path of awareness over obsession. By doing so, organizations and sales professionals can focus on their own strengths as they relate to the customer.

Do not let what you cannot do interfere with what you can do.

John Wooden

Summary

The planning process will lead you into productive markets and help you avoid unproductive ones. Understanding the main reason your customers use your product is invaluable in developing the message that you must articulate in order to consistently sell. Like a hiker beginning a climb, a marathon runner starting a race, or an entrepreneur founding a business, it is critical to not only create an initial plan but to routinely revisit your plan to meet changing conditions and re-examine assumptions.

Planning is a foundational activity that identifies your destination and the equipment needed to get you there. It produces four tangible deliverables:

> Written Goals
> Meaningful Value Message
> Initial List of Suspects
> Competitor Profiles

These documents will serve as planning resources for making better decisions, and facilitating better communications within your own company and with your prospects.

Do not be afraid to invest in a consultant. Engaging an expert to help you with your plan is money well spent. Fresh eyes can see opportunities that you are either too busy to see or have simply overlooked. You may have specific gaps in your process that need attention. A good consultant can help you address these without taking away from what you are already doing well.

Planning Exercises

Write your own obituary

Set sales goals

Develop meaningful value message(s)

Generate initial list of prospects

Profile top three competitors

Do something every day that you don't want to do; this is the golden rule for acquiring the habit of doing your duty without pain.

Mark Twain

PROSPECTING

Few words in the sales lexicon cause a salesperson to shudder as much as the word 'prospecting'. Images of awkward cold calls ending in failure and humiliation instantly leap to mind; the body becomes paralyzed with fear. Your palms begin to sweat and your stomach knots as you trade glances back and forth from your phone to your call list. Your throat goes dry, so you reach for a glass of water. Well, maybe it's not always that bad, but still prospecting the traditional way can be very unpleasant and unproductive.

The outcome of the prospecting activity will be an agreement between you and the new prospect to have a meeting to explore in detail the possibility of a fit between your product and the potential prospect's needs. The goal is to turn the potential prospect into a legitimate prospect. This may sound like a modest goal, and it certainly runs contrary to the traditional cold calling techniques that are well documented.

One Small Step

There is no order-asking involved in this stage, no fancy closing techniques, no spin or fast talk, simply a request for an agreement to a next qualifying meeting to explore the possibilities further. This is what will constitute a successful outcome in the prospecting activity, and will smoothly move us to the next phase. Many salespeople make the mistake of setting their goals for the prospecting phase unrealistically high. They tend to jump too far and too fast and ultimately defeat their chances of winning the deal in the long term. Traditional prospecting via cold calling is unpleasant for both the caller and the potential prospect.

Early in the tech boom of the 1990s it was common for prospects to identify themselves to vendors by requesting information from them. These folks essentially raised their hands and identified themselves as prospects. As these markets matured, the direct response prospect self-identification slowed dramatically. This cycle repeats itself as industries mature. Very few businesses can rely on prospects finding them as a means of survival. No salesperson or business can reach its full potential, or become The Selling Machine, without a solid prospecting methodology. In some cases, leads like this dried up almost completely. As a reaction to this, companies have been forced to find alternative sources of leads. Prospecting is the way to find these new leads. The goal of the prospecting activity is to convert potential prospects (also known as suspects) into legitimate ones.

The method of achieving the prospecting goal focuses on basic research and then making the best possible first impression by using contact techniques that are proven to work with the first warm contact.

Basic Research

Using the list of potential prospects that was developed within the planning activity, prioritize and build upon that basic information to form a better picture of the potential prospect. In addition to building upon your initial contact information, assemble three meaningful pieces of information about each potential prospect so that you will be able to approach them with some knowledge that will add to your credibility and improve your odds of success.

Most competition either does not do this at all, or spends too much time gathering irrelevant information. Once you know what to look for, you will be able to invest less than 15 minutes per potential prospect compiling this information. The kind of information we're talking about needs to have some relevance to your product. Use this information as you formulate your approach into the potential prospect. You will more than likely not use this information verbatim; instead, craft a message that is sensitive to the customer's point of view.

Specifically we want to capture:

> Contact Name
> Job Title
> Direct Phone Number
> Email Address

Most businesses have either most or all of this information on their public website. If you find it difficult to find the primary contact person, try other sources or just call in directly to the potential prospect business and simply ask. You will find that most receptionists are willing to help you, if you ask nicely.

To find the three meaningful pieces of information, the company's website again will be an excellent source, as most have press releases, annual reports, and stated corporate objectives. Items to look for include:

> Growth or Reduction Trends
> Physical Plant Expansions
> Changes in Leadership
> Mergers or Acquisitions
> New Products and Services
> Strategic Movement by Competitors

There are implications and inferences to be drawn from each of these items. Think to yourself what growth or reduction means to a company, a change in leadership to the employees, or a strategic move by one of their top competitors. You need to understand what effect these meaningful pieces of information will likely have on our potential prospect. Then, use your inferences to create a good opening with your initial warm contact.

Warm Contact

You've probably heard your parents say "It is not what you say, it is how you say it." This is so true. The Selling Machines knows that you can say almost anything as long as you say it the right way. The Selling Machine is not only aware of the tone used when saying something, but very carefully selects the right words to use. The combination of these approaches will take you from a 20% success rate in gaining a meeting to 80%.

Develop both oral and written contact templates that provide the best chance to move to the next phase —the qualifying call. The templates include items such as the Meaningful Value Message, developed during the planning stage, and industry-specific phrases and power statements gleaned from basic research. Good templates will set the hook in your effort to reel in the meeting. It is not uncommon to have multiple markets to sell into; therefore, multiple templates are needed. It is a good and efficient practice to plan prospecting activity so that you are calling into the same market or similar potential prospects for a period of time.

Take a specific item from one of the three meaningful pieces of information that we developed in our research activity, and present it in a way that it is not an affront to the prospect. This is exhibited in the example that follows.

Email Template

Here is a good warm email template with commentary added in blue. Use your own style and phrases while using the key elements shown as a guide. Reading scripts is a huge negative and a no-no for The Selling Machine. Phone conversations have a similar flow and overall content.

Jim,

Good afternoon and nice to meet you, albeit over email. My name is Laura Selzmore and I am responsible for business development for MilkTech. [This is a pleasant introduction and greeting].

I recently spoke with Mike Jones and he thought it would be appropriate if I sent you a note introducing myself. [Credibility statement: This statement establishes credibility because you have been referred.]

In short, MilkTech helps companies reduce production expenses. It is my understanding that you have an initiative or at least a desire to make some improvements in the near future regarding your milking equipment. Based on this and other research I have done on your company, I believe there may be a fit between what you need and what we provide. [Meaningful Value Message]

Would you be able to commit 15 minutes for a phone meeting to discuss in more detail? I would certainly appreciate it and also think it would be worthwhile. Below is my contact information. I also carry one of those blackberries, so I can be reached by email anytime. [Call to action: One small step!]

Connections, Connections and Connections

It's a well known saying in real estate, that the three key elements for success are, "location, location, and location." In sales, the three most important things are, "connections, connections and connections." As you approach your prospects, you need to think creatively about how to connect with them. Think about how you can connect with your prospect to establish credibility and move the process forward. Prospects who are not expecting to hear from you because they haven't asked you to call on them have little patience for an unconnected (cold) call.

There is a popular book and board game called "Six Degrees of Kevin Bacon." The premise is that everyone in the movies is connected to Kevin Bacon by no more than 6 degrees of separation. For instance, I may have a co-worker who once went to school with a person who works for a company that is a potential prospect of mine. This is an example of only two degrees of separation. A connection has been established. This personal connection is very powerful.

There are other types of connections that can be established. Commonality of industry, geography, or backgrounds can make decent connections. Though not as good as the personal connection, they can suffice to get a toe in the door. Take time at this warm contact stage to think creatively about how you will establish connection with your prospects. Old sayings get old because they're usually true and the old saying that you never get a second chance to make a first impression fits that description.

Summary

In-bound leads from referrals and self-identified prospects from advertising and other marketing activities cannot be relied upon exclusively. In order to succeed over the long term you must develop an active prospecting plan. Most salespeople fail at prospecting because they attempt to do too much. Setting your sights on achieving a next call is all that is important here. Credentials, entry message, and tone are the keys to success. Some background research must be done in order to succinctly communicate why a next meeting is worthwhile for the potential prospect. Think creatively about how to establish your warm connection. Wherever possible, play the detective game of finding a personal link to the individual with whom you are connecting. Because The Selling Machine always makes warm contact with the potential prospect, he generally achieves his objective.

Prospecting Exercises

Complete prospect profiles with basic research

Create warm contact email and phone templates

Draw a connection chain (Picture Wheel) to each of your potential prospects

It is better to know some of the questions than all of the answers.

                                        James Thurber

QUALIFYING

The qualifying stage is where you, the salesperson, become convinced that you have a product or service that can solve a genuine problem for a prospect, and you begin to develop an understanding of what that solution may be worth. Here you will uncover the motivation and interest level of your prospect. At the end of this stage, you will have a qualified prospect, a rough quantifiable business proposal, and an action plan to move forward.

Qualifying, simply put, is selling yourself on what you have to offer as a match to the customer's needs. In essence, you are establishing whether or not you are qualified to pursue the opportunity further. The stakes are high in this phase. Your credibility with the prospect, your understanding and preparedness will be on display. Qualifying is the most intimate phase because it is the first direct investment you and the prospect make together. A great performance at this stage will earn you the right to ask pertinent questions later.

Great Questions Make Great Salespeople

The primary tool employed in the qualifying stage is questioning. It sounds simple, but these questions must be designed to best uncover the answers you need to achieve momentum in proceeding further with this prospect. Because this is the first major impression with the customer, it's important that you take the time to uncover all the relevant information.

Everyone is familiar with the current state of the healthcare system in the U.S. Driven by deadlines and quotas, doctors rarely make the time for thorough diagnosis. Instead, patients get a two to five minute meeting that usually leads to the pharmaceutical solution du jour. The result is a hit or miss diagnosis that leaves the consumer feeling poorly served and a carousel ride to the check-out line or the next doctor.

Imagine you are going on a mountain climb. What information do you need to know to successfully navigate your way to the top? What are the weather conditions and trends? What anchors are in place? Are there sources of water along the way? Are there proven routes up the mountain? You get the picture.

As in all phases of selling, you must first have a detailed understanding of the terrain, and know what answers would constitute a positive or negative result, a go or no-go decision.

Picture Wheel

A good technique for developing these questions is the picture wheel. The picture wheel is a hub-and-spoke brainstorming technique designed to help you get your qualifying questions organized, so that you can find out as much as possible in as little time as possible. The hub represents your customer and the spokes represent important aspects of the account that, when fully explored, will give you a complete understanding or picture of the account. Like a good doctor, these questions will provide the basis for your diagnosis and eventual prescription.

Although there can be more, there will always be at least 4 major spokes in your Picture Wheel: Company Background, Main Reason, Approval Process, and Objections. Each of these spokes, or sails, will have branches that list clarifying questions designed to uncover the truth and, where appropriate, specific value.

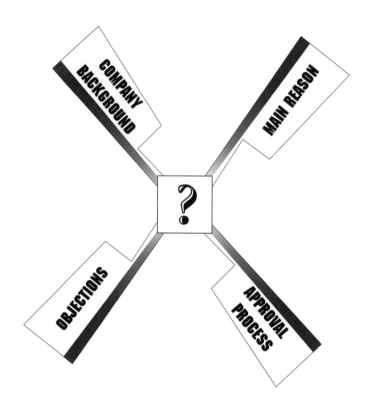

Very few of your competitors will ask GREAT questions. In fact, the quality of your questions will go a long way toward separating you from them. If through a series of very well phrased, probing questions you uncover the hidden opportunity in an account - perhaps something that your prospect was unaware of - then you may have already won the sale.

Let's take the doctor example. First, what are the answers that a doctor needs before recommending a cure? We know them almost by heart because every time we visit the doctor we are asked for 1) vital signs, 2) current symptoms, 3) personal and 4) family medical history. These are the four spokes of the doctor's picture wheel about us. In order to obtain the necessary information, you are first asked questions about your medical history and current condition. Usually this happens by you filling out some paperwork as you wait in the lobby. Then, a nurse will weigh you and then take your temperature and blood pressure. Essentially, she's asking your body questions. Finally, the doctor will ask you how you feel today, and the nature of your symptoms. These questions yield the answers that the doctor needs to make a diagnosis.

The lines of questioning that you develop using the Picture Wheel will form the heart of your initial qualifying call.

Anatomy of the Qualifying Call

The qualifying call is the second contact with the prospect. Remember that in the first call we simply gained a commitment from the prospect (one small step) to discuss the issue further. This qualifying call has six distinct elements: The opening, questioning, tone and feel, summary, agreement on next steps, and reality check. This anatomy is a flexible framework that allows you to efficiently obtain all the needed information. Most if not all qualifying activity can be done over the phone quicker and easier than in-person meetings. That said, this anatomy applies to both over-the-phone and in-person meetings.

Opening

The opening should be short and sweet. Include your name and company, and remind the prospect that you are calling as a follow up to your prior agreement. Be friendly, polite and professional. Show appreciation for the time that he is investing in this meeting. Leave room for your prospect to respond. Listen for hidden messages that can give insight into his frame of mind at the moment. If he is anxious, or hurried, you will be able to tell by the tone of his voice or body language.

It's important to understand the prospect's frame of mind during the meeting. If the prospect is distracted or in a negative frame of mind, consider re-scheduling the appointment. We're all human and we bring our emotions to the table. The Selling Machine is in tune with these issues as well as the pertinent facts. The end of the opening is a transition statement gaining permission to ask the necessary questions.

Questioning

Questions are the heart of qualifying. Here we will put the Picture Wheel in action to uncover the opportunity and value within the prospective account. You have done your homework and know not only the information you're looking for, but also the questions required to obtain it. You are well organized and can get there efficiently. The customer will know and feel this organization, and appreciate your professionalism.

The essential characteristics of great questioning include:

> Good Organization
> Open-ended
> Clarify Mystery Words
> Uncover Value Opportunities
> Open to Learning
> Opportunity to Build Rapport & Credibility

Where the average salesperson will skim the surface by asking overly broad questions, The Selling Machine will probe deeper to uncover real value. Here's an example of a good opening question.

> "Jim, I've done some research on Windmill Dairy. In your own words can you describe your most pressing business challenges as you see them?"

The question is broad, open-ended and immediately allows the customer to talk about his business, his role in the business, the challenges he faces, and anything else he wants to share. This question may provide answers that you will need without even having to ask them directly. This is the beauty of good open-ended questions. Another important bi-product is that the comfort level between the two of you will immediately improve. People love to talk about themselves. Let the prospect talk as long as he wants; the more he talks, the better.

> "Thanks, Jim. You've shared a lot of information that I didn't know. Would you be open to a few more questions that will help me determine if what I have to offer may be of value?"

Now, who could say no to that? Notice how as we move along we're asking permission to delve deeper. This builds trust and respect.

> "Jim, you mentioned that you have a lot of milking equipment that is in poor condition. Can you tell me how many pieces you have and what exactly you mean by poor?"

Fortunately for The Selling Machine, an average salesperson will ask a question and then write down the answer as given, even though the answer may not be specific enough. In this case, we've asked good clarifying questions designed to get closer to the truth. Jim will tell me exactly how many machines he has (not just "a lot") and will tell me (not just that the condition is "poor") but how old they are and how often they fail, how much they cost to repair and other relevant details that eventually lead me to understanding the value of my solution.

> "Jim, you told me that Windmill Dairy has 15 milking machines and that on average they are down for repair 20 hours per month each. How much would you say this costs your company per month in repairs and lost production?"

This is a Selling Machine question. We are now getting to the root of the business problem. How much does it cost and how much is it worth? That's the bottom line. You may have to help your prospect understand the actual costs by asking clarifying questions until you get to the root.

The final qualifying question should always be, "Is there anything else?" The reason for this question is to give the customer yet another opportunity to share additional information. It is not uncommon, given that you have gained more respect and rapport with the customer by this stage of the meeting, for the prospect to open up and share information that he may not share with the competition. As before, probe into the additional information with clarifying questions to make sure you understand not only the issue but also the value.

Tone and Feel

The tone of your questions, and the non-verbal signals exchanged during the qualifying process, is just as important as the words you use. As mentioned earlier, it's not always what you say, but how you say it. The impression you want the prospect to have about you is that you are sincere, genuinely interested, respectful, polite and professional. Overall, this builds the credibility and trust that is essential to earning the customer's business.

Key things to remember:

> Listen More than you Talk
> Demonstrate that you have Heard the Prospect
> Use Bridging Statements & Body Language
> Ask Permission to Delve Deeper & Go to Next Steps
> Confident but not Aggressive
> Professional but not Obtuse

Summarizing

The point of summarizing is to confirm with the customer that you understand the situation and have listened well to all that has been said. In the summary, restate the major content of the qualifying questions. Then, gain the customer's agreement that your understanding is accurate.

> "Jim, may I summarize to make sure I understand? You told me that you have 15 milking machines that are in poor condition that on average have 20 hours of

downtime per month each. We calculated that in downtime and repair, this situation costs Windmill Dairy $150,000 per quarter. Is that accurate?"

The above example represents one spoke in the Picture Wheel and takes a path in understanding the main reason and associated value with a single individual in the Windmill Dairy organization. Make sure you further develop the picture wheel by continuing down the path of all the spokes on the wheel with other people in the organization where appropriate.

Agreeing to Next Steps

Now that we have a solid picture of the prospect's issues and their associated value, it is time to establish what is the next step. The next step could very well be as simple as not moving forward at all. This is where many salespeople make the critical mistake of chasing a bad deal. This leads to wasted time and energy that could be better spent on another prospect. If after qualifying, it is clear that you have a solution to the issue, be confident in moving to the next stage.

Congratulations! You now have a qualified-prospect and quantifiable solution. All that is left is to agree on the next steps to the order.

"Jim, first of all, thanks for your time today. It has been very beneficial for me and I hope for you as well. I am certain that we have a solution for you. What in your mind are our next steps?"

Given all of the information you have obtained, it is now important to define and agree on the steps to the order or action plan. First, ask the prospect to outline the next steps. Do not assume that you know them. If the prospect seems disorganized or unsure, propose what the next steps should be, based on your experience.

Usually the qualified prospect offers some variation of the same steps that you have in mind; a presentation to the decision-making team, a proposal, and finally a closing agreement. Having the customer participate in the definition of the steps, helps solidify the timeline. Document it! This can be done formally in a document or in a simple email, as shown in the example below. The goal is for you and the qualified prospect to have a clear understanding of the path forward. This will ensure that you do not get ahead of your prospect. Here is an example action plan document and an email delivering it.

Next Steps Email

Jim,

Thanks for getting back to me and I hope you have a great weekend with your buddy from Atlanta. He'll be looking for some sunshine as it has been raining quite a bit this week in the South! As we discussed yesterday, I will be in meetings in Montreal next week but will be checking email and have my cell with me if you need me. [Pleasant greeting as always]

To be sure we are on the same page after yesterday's discussion, I wanted to send a rough draft of how I understand you will be proceeding. I want to understand your plan, so that I will be prepared, AND so I can make sure our resources are ready when you select us. Please review and let me know if I am on the right track. [Reason for the email clearly stated: Let's make sure we're on the same page]

1.You will meet next week with senior management to discuss the recommended next steps and "two" vendors to be considered.

2. After that, you will likely confirm your choice with "confirmatory due diligence" which includes calling references, company validation, etc.

3. After that, assuming you have your choice confirmed, you will solidify an agreement with the vendor.

4.Your goal is to have this completed ASAP in June, for your targeted July 1 kick off. [Steps to order clearly stated]

Jim, please let me know if I got anything wrong or am missing anything. Have a great weekend and hit'em well! [Call to action asks customer to confirm understanding]

Use the prospect's words wherever possible in the body of your note. "Confirmatory due diligence," for example were the prospects real words in this scenario. The tabular format below allows for more detail than the email. You can add columns for other information such as people responsible for item.

49

Action Item	Completion Date
Initial call to discuss Windmill Dairy business requirements	November
MilkTech to provide product material to Windmill Dairy	December
Presentation	Jan 4th
Follow up meeting to discuss results of presentation	Jan 6th
Conference call to review draft proposal	TBD (January)
Confirmatory due diligence	February
Vendor selection	February
Final proposal	February
Legal review of contract	February
Execution of contract	March
Project kickoff	March
Implementation	March through June
System Go-Live	June

Reality Check

Finally, conclude your qualifying session(s) with a reality check. Remind the now qualified prospect that you are confident you have a solution that will solve his problem and that you've both agreed to an action plan. Then, ask one final question:

> "Jim, as mentioned earlier, I'm confident that I have a solution that makes sense for you. If after we complete the action plan together and you too become convinced, do you see any reasons why MilkTech could not earn your business?"

This question will bring to the surface challenges that you will want to be aware of throughout the remainder of the sales cycle. In the chapter on closing, a section will be devoted specifically to handling these objections.

Summary

The qualifying step is the first occasion where the seller and the prospect make a joint investment in time. This is a pivotal step in the process so don't hurry it. Ask thoughtful (and thought-provoking) questions to uncover the information you need to convince yourself that you have a solution for the customer. It's a waste of effort and time to chase a deal that's not a good fit.

The quality of the questions will go a long way toward separating you from the competition. Knowing the anatomy of the qualifying call will add structure to your interaction with the prospect, and begin to instill confidence. The end result of the qualifying step is a qualified prospect. A qualified prospect is one with a problem you can solve, a desire to solve it, and the means to do so.

Now is the time to prove to this qualified prospect what the seller already knows, namely that he has the best solution.

Qualifying Exercises

Draw a picture wheel with major
qualifying questions

Write an example action plan with
steps to the order and dates

Create an email template that confirms
your understanding of Next Steps

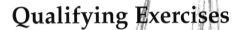

Believe one who has proved it. Believe an expert.

Virgil

———◦◦◦———

PROVING

Whereas in the qualifying stage the goal was to convince yourself that there is an opportunity worth pursuing, in the proving stage, the task is to convince the prospect that you have a solution worth buying. At the end of this stage, you will have a prospect that is not only a believer in your solution but also a partner going forward. You and the prospect will be in the same boat together, and the odds for closing the deal will have dramatically increased.

First, what is proof? For the answer, let's consult an authority (which is what this chapter is all about), the Oxford English Dictionary, to see how proof is defined. Its meaning will help us better understand how to deliver it.

> Proof- 1. That which makes good or proves a statement; evidence sufficient (or contribution) to establish a fact or produce belief in the certainty of something 2- the action, process, or fact of proving, or establishing the truth of, a statement; the action of evidence in convincing the mind; demonstration.

The challenge is to effectively deliver compelling evidence that answers the buyer's main reason for purchase. How do you do this? Every prospect becomes a customer because at some point they become convinced that there is a return on their investment and a means to get there. In the proving stage, the focus will be on the "R" in Return on Investment. This is done because the investment only makes sense once the return is established as real and beneficial. The selection of the best form, or combination of forms, for delivering the proof will increase your effectiveness. Finally, the Proof Matrix is a tool that marries the buyer to the desired return, and method of proof, to create a coherent and effective strategy.

Focus on the 'R'

Too often, salespeople present an investment proposal without adequately addressing the expected return. The Selling Machine focuses on the "R." The Return has to be specific to the buyer. In a sales campaign, sell at multiple levels and to multiple people. Each individual has their own buying perspective. In others words, every person involved in the buying decision has their own idea of what constitutes return on investment. The Selling Machine recognizes this and uncovers each buyer's "R" during the qualifying stage and then presents proof to match it. Remember that the "R" is what motivates the prospect to buy.

For example, in a complex business sale, the approval process means being involved with several buyers at many levels and in some cases even buying committees. Recognize that each of these individuals has their own "R" and that they may be quite different from one another. Although there may be common "R"s at the various levels, get specific within the individual deal you are working. Typically, an end-user-level buyer is concerned with functional issues such as ease of use and simplification of workload. Your challenge is to apply your proving activities specifically to that buyer. It is not enough to say that your solution is easy to use and reduces workload. You must prove it.

As you move up the buying hierarchy, this same principle applies. In the same deal, you may encounter a VP-level buyer like the VP of Operations. The "R" for this buyer may involve operational issues that can vary considerably. Some examples are which customer satisfaction, response amd delivery times, and budget, among others. The challenge for this VP is to implement without disrupting current operations.

From a senior executive perspective, factors such as shareholder value, financial performance, strategic direction and regulatory compliance may be paramount. Specifically, financial issues may include earnings per share (EPS), market share, growth and expansion, return on assets, equity, and profitability. Regulatory compliance examples may include accounting rules such as Sarbanes-Oxley; manufacturing guidelines for quality like ISO or CMMI; safety and environmental rules such as ISO, FDA, EPA, Hazmat and OSHA.

Understanding the level of the buyers that need to be convinced, and their respective motivation will allow you to present and prove your solution in the most effective manner. The Selling Machine understands the specific return for each individual, and then proves their solution in the best format for that individual. Now let's take a look at the six forms of proof that comprise your proof arsenal.

Proof Arsenal

Presentation is the simplest form of proof. There are several types of presentations. Most think of a formal setting, such as a boardroom meeting, or a meeting that incorporates a power point or slide presentation. Other examples include teleconference calls, form letter documents, or simple one-on-one meetings, independent of props. Regardless of the manner of presentation, all share the same elements, which include the specific return related to the main reason for each buyer. In other words, tailor the presentation to your audience. Only present pertinent information to the buyers at hand. Do not present proof that does not affect the buyer to whom you are presenting. For example, it's usually a waste of time and effort to present regulatory features and benefits to an end user. Focus on what the buyers at hand care about!

A presentation is a statement of confidence. It says to the prospect that you understand the return at each buyer level, and that you can deliver the solution. The presenter's style, clothes, manners, voice, energy and confidence levels all make a huge impression. A simple presentation may suffice in some cases as the only form of proof needed. In other cases, depending on the degree of risk, cost, urgency, reputation and other factors, the simple presentation must be augmented by other forms of proof.

A very powerful form of proof is *a third party* validation. A third party might be an independent source such as industry or financial analysts, media reports, and magazine articles. It can be awards that your company has won. Certain levels of buyers respond to these types of sources as they are considered to be objective and unbiased. Objectivity provides comfort and a level of detail that cannot be obtained directly from the seller or other sources. They also instill confidence in the buyer because they speak to issues like credentials, reputation, financial stability, and quality in a believable fashion. It is recommended that you develop and use them routinely as part of your proof arsenal.

To *demonstrate* is to show or exhibit that which you are selling. Demonstrations are very often employed as a form proof. Seeing is believing, as the saying goes and often telling is not enough. The prospect prefers to see, but some products, such as professional services, insurance, and securities do not lend themselves to demonstration. In these cases, the proof will focus on the mannerisms, behavior, experience, knowledge, and professionalism of the sales presenter.

The demonstration shows that what you have said about your solution is true. The Selling Machine is not sidetracked by an endless catalog of features and benefits, but focuses on the individual buyer's main reason. Allow prospects to touch, ask questions about or even "test drive" the offering. The more concrete the solution becomes, the more likely it is to be believed.

The *business assessment* is a formal exercise between the prospect and the seller, where the initial findings from the qualifying stage are validated. Most often, the end result is a quantifiable estimation that is presented in a format that supports the expected return from the product or solution. Typically associated with more complex sales, the assessment serves to provide a more detailed instrument of proof that resonates not only with the company in general, but also with the specific levels of buyers. By its nature, the assessment is a significant investment in time, sometimes money, as well as resources. For the complex sale, it can be an investment worth making.

The *reference* derives its proof power by being a real life example that the prospect can visualize. In any major deal it is essential to provide references. This is where The Selling Machine shines because, as mentioned before, he understands that customers are his most valuable resource. Here he will use that resource to the fullest. References provide an observable proof of concept for your prospects, and, in a way the salesman cannot, confirm the effectiveness of your solution. The prospect relates to the reference like no other form of proof because the reference has walked in the prospect's shoes.

As mentioned previously, your customers are your most valuable resource. Fulfilling your commitments to customers and bringing value to them will ensure that they are available to help grow your business. References must be cultivated.

The choice of the reference is an important one. First, match buyer levels as much as possible between the reference and the prospect. Executives like to compare notes with other executives, VPs prefer to network with other VPs and so on. It's natural that this is the case because their Rs have more in common. Additionally, the choice of which particular reference account to use should be carefully considered. Consider the prospect's industry and competitive landscape, so that you make the wisest choice. Be aware that the wrong selection here may cost you the deal.

In government markets, the sharing of information between peers is usually relatively easy—certainly more so than commercial and industrial ones. Therefore, the choice of reference that matches most closely in terms of size and location usually works. Look for model government entities that others tend to emulate and be sure to pursue those opportunities.

What do you do if you don't have a reference in a specific market? That's a great question, because as you expand your business you have to look for markets in which you don't yet have a customer. How do you approach these situations in terms of providing a reference as proof that your solution works? The key here is to use your knowledge of your customer accounts and your imagination to parlay the customers you have in certain markets to new customers in other markets, looking for commonalities. For instance, if you have customers in the hotel industry but none in the hospital industry, you have to ask yourself what these two industries have in common. You will be surprised at how much commonality you can find.

In industry, where competition is most brutal, you must be aware of the buyer's psychology to avoid potential pitfalls. Certain companies consider themselves leaders in their field. Usually there is a handful in each industry. This creates a highly competitive environment where rivalries are white hot. It may be that one of your customers has four major rivals. On the surface, your customer may appear to be a perfect fit as a reference because of all the commonality but, because of the competitive landscape, the opposite may be true. For instance, if one of your available references is Heinz, an introduction to Hunt's may be the proverbial kiss of death. Certain companies insist on doing things differently from their rivals in order to differentiate themselves, and they don't want to share trade secrets.

The effectiveness of your reference will depend on your expertise in selecting the right fit. You need to match the right individuals with the best accounts possible in order to make the greatest impact.

The final form of proof is known alternately as a *sample, trial, or pilot.* This form puts your product or service into the hands of the prospect so that he can convince himself that the solution works. Some products lend themselves easily to this type of proof where others do not. Typically, the more expensive the item, the more cautious the seller must be in making it available.

That said, there can be a place for it even in large deals where the controls and expectations have been carefully set. From a buyer psychology standpoint, the actual use of the solution in a real-world setting that is specific to that buyer can be decisive. Recommend a short trial to prevent undue delay in the sales cycle. A short fixed period adds emphasis and urgency.

Proof Matrix

So far in this chapter The Selling Machine has discussed focusing on the return portion of ROI and matching that to the individual buyer as well as various forms of proof in your arsenal. The proof matrix combines all this detail into a single table that makes executing the strategy simpler. Now let's look at a business-to-business (B2B) proof matrix, incorporating the items discussed so far.

Level	Main Reason	The "R"	Proof Arsenal
CEO	Financial	Profit	Presentation, Reference
VP	Customer Satisfaction	Satisfaction index	Third Party, Trial
User	Simplify Work	Easy to use	Demonstration, Reference

Bear in mind that this matrix is not just applicable to business-to-business sales but can also be used on higher-end consumer sales. Compare how the purchase of a car may look when displayed on a proof matrix.

Level	Main Reason	The "R"	Proof Arsenal
Dad	Economy	Affordable payment	Presentation, Third Party
Mom	Style and Convenience	Attractive and practical	Reference, Trial
Kids	Fun	Entertainment	Demonstration

Others have written extensively about personality types of buyers and this is something you may want to explore. Decision styles vary from Analytical types to Drivers. It's worth considering the personality types of your prospects as you determine the most effective proof for each individual.

Summary

As The Selling Machine, you are credible because you can prove your solution. By focusing on the "R," choosing the most effective form of proof for the given situation and then matching this to your individual buyer, you ensure buy-in from your prospect, making them partners in the remaining stages of the deal. Don't move past this stage until you know that you've proved it. Be aware that the prospect may not admit that he is convinced in order to create a negotiating posture, but those situations are rare and okay regardless. Ask your prospect, "Based on what you've seen and heard, have I proved to you that what we have will do the job?" Really listen to the reply. You may have to revisit your proof arsenal before moving on. The prospect's confirmation brings you that much closer to your sale. Now that both the prospect and you are convinced, let's discuss the stage of the deal that pops "The Big Question."

Proving Exercise

Create a Proof Matrix for one of your
qualified prospects matching:

Buyer Level

Main Reason

Specific Return

Form of Proof

That which costs little is less valued.

Miguel de Cervantes

PROPOSING

Do you remember the moment you asked your beloved to marry you, or vice versa? Do you remember where you proposed and all the details surrounding it? Perhaps even the exact words of the proposal? Did you rehearse the exact words? Chances are that you do, and you did. If you've never popped the big question, try to remember another important big question that you asked or a decision you asked someone to make. Important occasions where you ask the big questions are certainly memorable. Sales situations are just like that, and the stage where the big questions get formally asked is called proposing.

At the end of the proposing phase, you will have delivered a document or articulated a specific proposal to the qualified prospect. The previous stages of The Selling Machine have equipped you with the knowledge to make a complete proposal specific to the prospect's needs. Because you have qualified your prospect well, and then proved to him that what you have meets his requirements, you are now in a position to put together a proposal from which the customer can place an order. At the end of the proposing stage, you will have delivered a specific and convincing proposal on which the customer can act. You will finally have popped the big question, and will have possibly even gotten the big YES for an answer!

Articulate the Strategy

By this stage in the process, you should have gathered enough specific information about your customer to articulate a rationale for a business relationship or deal. The common mistakes that most people make at this stage fall into two categories: Too little detail or too much.

On the one hand, salespeople will rely too heavily on published marketing material, and brochures, making the proposal too general or boilerplate. In this case, the salespeople will package a simple quote sheet along with this material and present it to their prospect as a proposal. There are occasions where this approach will work. For example, with an existing customer when there is not a big need for detail. Or, where the item you are selling is relatively inexpensive. In these instances, it may make sense to package general marketing material along with a price sheet with the important addition of a strategy statement in the cover letter.

At the other extreme, usually in complex sales, a common mistake is to provide so much detail that the underlying strategy gets lost. In certain deals, the response format is already prescribed by the customer such as in a request for proposal (RFP) or competitive bid. In these scenarios, you must still place a clear strategy statement in a cover letter in your response. In complex sales where the response format is not prescribed, be careful not to allow the detail to dilute the underlying strategy. Most deals will fall between these two extremes with freedom to create and place your own strategy statement.

The right mix is a strategy statement with a plan of action designed to accomplish specific goals. It begins with a statement of the prospect's business issues (probably no more than five) which you uncovered during the qualifying phase, aligned with the solution your company provides. Use your customer's prioritization of these business issues in the organization of the statement. The strategy statement is set forth in the cover letter immediately following the salutation. Since it is placed in the cover letter, the strategy statement must be clear, refined, and concise. Think of this placement as your project slogan. Later on in the executive summary, and elsewhere in the proposal, you will elaborate. The strategy must include: what you will do, why you will do it, how you will do it, why are you uniquely qualified to deliver it, and the expected result.

Anatomy of the Proposal

The most important thing about the proposal, is the articulation of the expected benefits paired with clearly defined deliverables. The proposal is an instrument that the prospect uses to take the necessary action to place an order and become a customer. It should be compelling, logical and easily understood. Be specific in your proposal. Remember, general propositions are no good. Not all proposals must be written, and not all written proposals must be complex. The size of the deal and your track record with the account will dictate which medium to use. Let's now break down the six most important components of a written proposal.

Cover Letter

The Cover Letter is a business form letter on your company letterhead, which consists of four major elements: gratitude statement, project slogan, credentials, and a call to action. Usually less than a page, this component is short and sweet. In today's world, this is often an email.

Executive Summary

Of all the proposal elements, the Executive Summary is the most critical. The Executive Summary identifies a problem worth solving and establishes that you are qualified to solve it. The Executive Summary is usually no more than one page, and always includes: background events, a description of the opportunities found, and your company credentials.

The Executive Summary succinctly adresses the customer's current business issues, outlines the plan to address these issues, and the estimated ROI which will result. Using facts uncovered during the qualifying phase, describe the situation as it exists today and paint a word picture of how this project will improve it. You want to impress upon the reader the investments in time that you and the prospect have made together in formulating this solution.

Return on Investment

The ROI is where the rubber meets the road. This is what catches the prospect's attention, because it is what he cares about the most. For this reason, it should be placed near the beginning of the proposal. Details about your findings should be expressed in both hard numbers and soft benefits. If you look back to the qualifying stage, recall that the dairy prospect had two major areas of opportunity, production downtime and maintenance expense. This is precisely where you will find the financial return data. Below is an example of these areas of opportunity.

Area of Opportunity	Findings	Cost	Financial Return
Production Downtime	60 hours per quarter	$30,000 per quarter	$15,000 per quarter
Maintenance Expense	$120,000 per quarter	$120,000 per quarter	$60,000 per quarter
		$150,000 per quarter	**$75,000 per quarter**

In addition to the hard economic benefits, there are invariably soft benefits which do not neatly yield quantifiable economic returns. For example, the elimination of unwanted downtime can be neatly tied to associated dollars, and so is a hard benefit whereas freeing staff for other vital areas is less tangible. Other examples of soft benefits include:

Improved Work Environment
Customer Satisfaction
Deferred Hiring
Space & Time Efficiencies
Opportunity Cost
Risk Management
Quality Standards
Employee Morale

Soft benefits have added weight when you are dealing with regulated industries and government entities; for example, meeting FDA requirements. Your solution possibly assists with maintaining compliance, but unless there is a penalty or fine, it is very difficult to assign a meaningful economic return. The benefit is nonetheless real.

If a cost comparison for alternative or competitive offerings is available, you can include that in this section as well.

Investment Options

Customers need and want options. Your proposal should present multiple options that cover a range of costs, timing, and deliverables. Sometimes one alternative may suffice. In other cases three to five choices may be appropriate. Beware of slicing the bread too thin. Providing options may eliminate the need to negotiate, depending on the experience of your buyer. At a minimum, these options will set a framework for any negotiation that may follow. Lastly, every proposal you make should have an expiration date.

Conclusion

The conclusion will correlate the investment to the return. Projects are funded and prioritized based on expected returns with an emphasis on financials. By specifically stating the anticipated payback period, and thus making the return seem more tangible, you will see your prospect become more enthusiastic about the project and the investment.

Attachments

Attachments belong at the end of the proposal. This is where you are going to place necessary details and complementary materials that may not have been positioned in the main body of the proposal.

References
Customer Stories
Contract Terms
Resumes
Timelines
Specifications
Illustrations

Delivery and Timing

You should only go through the effort of developing a formal proposal once you and your prospect are both convinced that the opportunity is viable. If you preempt, you will have wasted your time, and hurt your position in the deal. Warning: sometimes a customer will act unconvinced as a negotiating ploy. The buying psychology at work goes something like this: if I can get the salesperson to doubt the value of his offering, or the fit, or some other element, then the salesperson will immediately drop the price and give us a huge bargain. Be aware of this buying psychology, so that you can react appropriately.

Before you go to press on your proposal, test it out on your champion or sponsor at the prospective customer's business, or if you are not certain of that source, get peer review. In any case—run it up the flag-pole first. Present your proposal first as a draft and label it as such. Do a verbal walk through, dress rehearsal before finalizing. Once you're convinced it's ready, then it is best to deliver the document in person or at least walk your prospect through it over the phone to make sure it makes sense.

Summary

Pop the question the right way at the right time. You have earned the right to ask for the order. Make it understandable and don't bury the question deep in the proposal. Have a flexible template that you can mix and match to suit the deal. This will save you time. Test your proposal on a friendly contact within the organization to see if it makes sense and to identify gaps. Proposing should only be done when the groundwork has been properly laid. Like the good doctor we can't propose a solution until we understand the problem.

Proposing Exercise

Write a complete proposal incorporating:

Cover Letter

Executive Summary

Return on Investment

Investment Options

Conclusion

Attachments

Let what will be said or done, preserve your sangfroid immovably, and to every obstacle, oppose patience, perseverance, and soothing language.

Thomas Jefferson

CLOSING

If you do not immediately receive an order after the proposing stage, it is because the prospect either has an objection or wishes to negotiate. It's that simple and it is common. Most large deals will enter this phase, and it is critical that you not panic. The closing section of this book will equip you with the tools you need to maintain your cool when the customer presents obstacles at the close of the selling process.

Your mindset should be that objections and negotiations are natural. Prepare a list of common objections and negotiating points so that you are not caught off guard. Negotiations can be viewed as a specific type of objection. There are golden rules you should understand before you negotiate. Finally, after the sale, how you manage the account will go a long way to determining whether the customer you land becomes a mere transaction or a part of your Selling Machine. Close the right way, by not treating the order as an end, rather as a new beginning.

Overcoming Objections

Any response other than 'yes' from a customer is an objection. Objections are simply items that keep you from the order. Sometimes they are substantial, but most of the time they are merely a buyer's reflex. Identify and isolate the true objection, so that you can respond effectively. Get all of the objections out on the table before addressing any single one. This will limit the iterations of endless and vague objections, thus shortening the sales cycle. Once you have them all out on the table, have the prospect prioritize the list. Then begin to address each one in turn beginning with the most important. You will find that those objections at the bottom of the list will simply fade away.

Approaching an objection hypothetically is a great way to get them all out on the table. For example, if the prospect's objection is, "I need my manager to approve", the way to handle this is by simply asking hypothetically, "If your manager approves, would you be on board?" Turn objections into questions. For instance, a prospect might say "We can't go forward until Bill sees it." Your reply should be "What does Bill need to see?" Every objection should be met head on and followed up with, "What else?" Make sure you understand the objection and write it down. Repeat it back to the prospect and have him confirm. Finally, take the prescribed action to satisfy the objection. Here is the objection cycle in a nutshell.

1. Understand the objection by asking clarifying questions and restating it.
2. Have prospect confirm that the deal cannot go forward without addressing the issue AND that you (The Selling Machine) fully understand it.
3. Ask if there are any other issues: "What else?"
4. Prioritize objections if there is more than one.
5. Clarify each objection with a question.
6. Take the necessary action to overcome it.

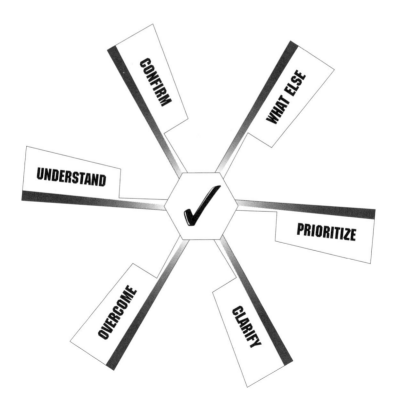

Anticipating common objections, and having a pre-pared response will help you close more deals. Create a list of common objections in one column and the best possible responses in the adjacent column. Working through a group exercise is a great way to build this list. Below is a sample:

Objection	Clarification	Response
We're concerned about your company's financials.	What specifically about the financials concerns you? Who is concerned?	Provide a financial report. Set up a call with your CFO or President.
My manager needs to approve.	In these situations, what does your manager typically like to see?	Provide what is asked for and if possible have a dialog with the manager
The competitor is less expensive.	Provide list of your strengths	Which competitor? What offering?

The good news is that most objections are straight-forward, and can be easily overcome. There are a few, however, that may prove to be too difficult to over-come in the short term. Examples of these fatal objec-tions include: corporate buyouts, personal illness, and some organizational changes. Recognize these for what they are, and be prepared to react. In these cases, you may have to go back to an earlier stage and begin with a new contact. Look for guidance from your con-tact, and don't give up until you're sure it's absolutely dead.

If you get too many or too few objections, it's probably

a sign that you did not do an adequate job in the proving phase. You may have proceeded to the proposing stage too early. Take a step back and revisit your proof arsenal. It's preferable to go back when the circumstances dictate than to proceed like a blind bulldog. Don't get frustrated. Instead, recognize the situation and move forward like a professional.

Negotiating

Negotiating should be fun. It is a game, and your goal is to win the game and preserve your proposal. Games are only fun, however, if you know the rules. The purpose of this section is to familiarize you with these rules. Before you negotiate, you must first confirm that you have been selected. Do not negotiate too early! Very good buyers will always leave two competitors in the game even if they are certain they know who they want to buy from. Your goal is to not let this happen.

In the proposing stage, you delivered several options to your prospect. By varying different price points, terms and conditions, and deliverables, you have created choices. This will serve as your base of negotiation as well as serve as your first response to their request for a concession. Never bid against yourself and do not treat it like an auction.

You must do your homework, just as you did in developing your common objections and responses. Make a list of high and low value items for both you and your customer. What is a low value item to you may be a high value item to your prospect, and vice versa. Negotiating, then, is simply trading these items. For each item the prospect receives, the seller should receive something too. It's not a "give" but a trade. Brainstorm to create your list. Here are a few common examples of sellers high and low value items:

High Value	Low Value
Sales Price	Payment Terms
Publicity	Length of Contract
Referrals	Warranty

You want to try and understand what your prospect's list of high and low value items look like. Whenever possible, you want to trade items that are of low value to you but that have a high value to your prospect, for items that are of high value to you but low value to the prospect. Consider this list of customer items:

High Value	Low Value
Payment Terms	Sales Price (to an extent)
Long Term Agreement	Publicity
Reliability	Referrals

Notice how the customer's priorities are almost the mirror opposite of yours. The negotiation win-win in this situation is obvious. We can retain price integrity and still get publicity and referrals in exchange for our commitments on payment terms, long term agreement, and extended warranty. Before making any concessions in a negotiation, you should first know (or at least have a strong clue) what your prospect's high and low value items look like.

A classic mistake that many salespeople make is to try and close the deal by conceding instead of trading. The reason this approach doesn't work is that once you've conceded something without getting anything in return, the message you send is negative. You're saying that the concession is unimportant and so imply that you have more to give, thus extending the negotiation. You're sending the signal that you have more to give. A good buyer will then ask for more.

Allow me to use a personal example to illustrate. My dearly beloved wife convinced me to join her on a trip to our local jeweler. The local jeweler is a very nice man and a fine artist and craftsman. Naturally, my wife had done her homework and picked out the ring that she "had to have." I, acting as buyer, told the jeweler that we liked the ring and wanted it except that the price needed to be better. Specifically, I asked the jeweler for a 25% discount. Almost immediately, the jeweler said yes to a 25% discount. Can you guess what my feeling was about him accepting this offer? The answer is not obvious, but does make sense psychologically. Because he said yes and asked for nothing in trade, I felt like the deal wasn't good enough. Instinctively, until we are either told 'no' or are asked for something in return, we don't feel like we've gotten the best deal possible.

Golden Rules

There are many books dedicated to negotiating. So it is unnecessary for us to cover every nuance. That said, The Selling Machine incorporates proven negotiation principles into the selling process. Below are the golden rules of negotiation that are proven to work:

Don't Negotiate Until you are Selected
Don't Bid Against Yourself
Don't Give Without Getting
Do Respond with Choices
Rarely (almost never) use "Take It or Leave It"
Trade Low Value Items for High Value Items
Defend your Initial Position First
Invite a Counter Offer (preferably in writing)
Promise Only that you Will Consider the Offer
Know your Competition
Know your Limits
Be Prepared to Walk Away

Account Management

The best way to close the right way is to avoid closing the wrong way. Don't ever close with tricks or dishonesty. Anything gained in the short-term will be lost double in the long-term. Persist without being obnoxious. Be someone the customer wants to be associated with long-term by being someone you would like to be associated with long-term. This is the essence of good account management.

Encourage and inspire. Feed and nurture your customers by helping them in unexpected ways. Train yourself to actively look for information that your customer can use to help him do his job better or even in his personal life. Be reliable and follow through after the sale to make sure your company is delivering on its commitments. Don't disappear at the first sign of a problem. Don't ever disappear. There will be problems and you need to be available to directly address them. More than anything, account management is about character and integrity more than any specific technique.

Be authentic and true to yourself. Leave acting to the stage. It is true that you want to be fun, interesting and polite, but above all else, be yourself. Putting on an act will never work for very long. Staying engaged after the sale will win you valuable points with the customer and separate you from your competitors. Dividends will be paid when you go back to your customer for future sales and references. Healthy relationships within a particular department have the potential to expand your existing footprint and create more business in other departments or locations of that same customer. Think how this customer, if treated well, can help you connect to other potential business.

Routine follow-up after the sale and addressing problems early and directly will preserve your most valuable asset, the customer, and ensure that your most precious resource is a renewable one. When was the last time you called a customer? Do it now.

Summary

Encountering obstacles at the close of a sales cycle is natural. Do not panic. Recognize the response as either an objection that needs addressing or an attempt to begin negotiations. Be prepared to answer common objections that satisfy your prospect's issue. Always get confirmation that the objection has been handled and if there are any other outstanding issues. Negotiations are natural. Do not assume that a negotiation will cost you something. In fact, it may make the deal larger! Again, be prepared. Know what is important to you and your customer and what is not. Make a list and be prepared to trade. Finally, stay engaged with your customer after the sale. Be as available after you've made the sale as when you were pursuing the sale. The secret to The Selling Machine is how you treat your most important and renewable resource!

Closing Exercises

Draft objections list and ideas for
overcoming each one

Identify low and high value items for
you and your customer

Time the destroyer is time the preserver.

T.S. Eliot

CONCLUSION

If you think selling is easy, then you probably have never earned your living as a salesperson. Selling is work, hard work! The Selling Machine gives a context and direction for that work so that you can get the most out of it! Use The Selling Machine and become The Selling Machine!

What we do with our time is what separates the successful from the mediocre, the strivers from the easily satisfied. It is important to understand the sales cycle not just in terms of chronological time but in events and milestones. The six phases of The Selling Machine represent the critical events and milestones in the selling process. There are various ways to align time and people with the selling tasks to produce the most effective and efficient selling machine for you and your organization. Marketing and Inside Sales (or even a third party) may be able to accomplish the first three opening stages (planning, prospecting and qualifying) while Outside Sales works the closing activities (proving, proposing and closing).

Or, in an organization where you are basically left to fend for yourself, you will have to manage your day in such a way that you perform all the tasks as efficiently as possible. In these cases, it helps to invest whole blocks of time on a particular activity instead of moving back and forth between them. Think 'planning week' or 'prospecting day' where you spend an entire day or week on a particular step. This type of work plan helps because the more focused time you spend on something, the better you become at it. You develop a rhythm by doing something over and over again. Skirting from one activity to another is inefficient.

Using The Selling Machine methodology you can quantify your performance and pipeline using these five key selling metrics:

New Suspects Identified
Qualifying Calls Made
Qualified Prospects
Proposals Delivered
Sales Made

Every sales activity you undertake belongs to one of the six stages of The Selling Machine. Indeed, if what you are doing does not belong in one of the six stages then you are not selling! Add to your storehouse of knowledge by inserting into the various phases complementary material. There are many experts who delve deeply into specific areas. As you grow and refine your knowledge of the science of selling, your success will grow also.

It has been said, and of course it's true, that we all have the same amount of time at our disposal every day. Time is democratic. No one is born with more time in a day than anyone else. How we manage our time seriously impacts our success or failure as sales-people. Incorporate time management into your planning process and use the time you have to set The Selling Machine in motion!

Who do those guys think they are anyway;
trying to write a book?

Olivia Cannon

———— ✺ ————

ACKNOWLEDGMENTS

We gratefully acknowledge the many authors and experts that have influenced our careers in general and this work in particular. Because of the nature of knowledge, it is nearly impossible to give complete credit in all cases. This is surely the case with us and for any omission of credit we extend our sincerest apologies.

Certain authors and books have influenced our careers and shaped our thinking. Authors that we recommend include: Al Ries, Zig Ziglar, and Stephen Covey. Classic works such as: <u>How to Win Friends and Influence People</u>, <u>SPIN Selling</u>, <u>Secrets of Closing the Sale</u> and <u>The Art of Negotiating</u> are 'must-reads' for the sales professional. We recommend all these works and authors to you for further reading and study.

We also encourage you to read business books in general to add to your knowledge base. Whether you read sales-specific books, general business books, biographies or whatever, your knowledge base is a resource to your customers and differentiates you from your competitors. Never stop learning!

It has taken both a great deal of inspiration and support to write this book. When the three of us first undertook this project we each provided our own forecast of the length of time it would take to complete.

Some of us said it would take only a matter of months and others of us said it would take years. It's not appropriate here to point fingers at the overly optimistic, suffice it to say that the actual investment in time was closer to the second estimate.

That being the case, it required enormous patience on the part of our families. We want, especially, to thank our wives and children for allowing us to borrow weekends from time to time. The publication of this book is proof that these weekends were not entirely recreational boondoggles. Thank you, Ladies! We also want to thank our friends who provided getaway retreats for us. We want to acknowledge our Hiawassee and Caesar's Head friends for providing inspirational settings in which to do our work. Without the support of our family and friends The Selling Machine simply would not have been possible.

We're also indebted to our reviewing team who provided critical input and corrections prior to submission. Lisa Anderson, Todd Lorbach, Jack Peyrouse, Lewis Tollison, Mark Vetzel, and Meredith Kinsey, each made time to read and offer suggestions that helped make it better than it otherwise would have been. Finally, thanks to Joel Hochman and the Publishing Machine at Arbor Books for believing in the book and for making the final product better than we ever thought it could be. A special thanks goes to Ashley Kehoe for her design and layout work. She was diligent, professional and a lot of fun to work with as were all the folks at Arbor.

THE AUTHORS

Michael Pace has held a number of executive positions in sales and sales management, primarily targeting the emerging Latin American market. He is currently Vice President of Inside Sales for Datastream Systems. Michael is a graduate of Wofford College.

Landy Wingard, a graduate of The Citadel, began his career in software and telecom sales with MCI before joining Datastream Systems in 1996 as a Corporate Sales Executive and Sales Manager.

Michael Cannon has held a variety of sales, sales management, and executive positions in software, telecom and internet companies. He is founder of PWC Group, a Greenville, South Carolina based sales consultancy. Michael is a graduate of Washington and Lee University.

The authors have worked together as a solutions-oriented team for more than a decade. Each has "carried a bag" and knows exactly what it means to own a number.

PWC GROUP

PWC Group is a sales consulting firm founded by Michael Cannon and located in Greenville, SC. The company's goal is to become the preferred sales resource for businesses by delivering solutions that bring tangible value in the form of increased sales. It does so by delivering a full set of services including sales training, consulting, outsourced business development and special projects.

PWC Group's experts have trained literally hundreds of successful salespeople. Instruction can be in either seminar format or one-to-one. The basis for PWC training is its proprietary six-step sales methodology called The Selling Machine. The Selling Machine teaches a disciplined and managed sales process that can be tailored to clients' specific requirements.

The outsourced business development service, also known as the Virtual Selling Machine℠, solves a fundamental dilemma for small and medium-sized firms that want to grow their business without adding expensive sales overhead. PWC Group's Virtual Selling Machine℠ complements a company's sales approach with a fully outsourced or supplemental model.

Additional information on PWC Group is available at www.pwcsales.net.